LAUGHTER:
THE BEST MEDICINE

Tara S. Dickherber, LPC, NBCCH

Illustrations by Steve Meritt
Graphic and Cover Design by Tracy Brooke

Contents

Acknowledgments

This book is dedicated to my hubby and my munchkin-thanks for your patience, support, smiles, and laughter through it all!

It may be short and sweet but there's a tribe of people who helped me get this book done. I want to start with my dear friend and mentor Courtney Armstrong. Without your encouragement, understanding, guidance, and faith in me this book would still be scribbles on post it notes. A thank you to Mary Meritt for your editing professionalism. You took my ramblings and created order and sense of them. To Steve Meritt thank you for taking my words and putting them into pictures. I said for a while if I wrote a book it had to have pictures too! Let me not forget Tracy Brooke of Giant Leap Productions. I don't know how you do the graphics you do, nor do I know how you see into my head and create the graphics of my writer's dream but you did it. You took everything that everyone did and pulled it all together into a book I'm excited to put out into the world. So thank you. Bill O'Hanlon; thank you for your wonderful webinar on writing and getting published! And lastly thanks to all my other friends, cohorts, and even clients. It takes a tribe of amazing people to support a writer along her or his journey to publication! I truly am blessed with a fabulous and funny tribe!!

Humor: My Superpower!

Introduction

"One of the best things that binds us as a family is a shared sense of humor."- Ralph Fiennes

Welcome to my very first prescription non-fiction book ever. We all have to have a first, - first job, first client in private practice, first love; so this is my first prescription non-fiction book. I greatly appreciate you purchasing this book and taking the time to read it! Let me give you a little insight into why this book even happened.

This whole thing really got started because friends were bugging me to write a book about hypnosis and weight loss. Weight loss? That's something my husband helps his clients with in his office, but not something I work with in my office. Long story short it planted a seed that grew into this. I know a lot of authors will slip into their books a résumé so to speak of their accomplishments, licenses, etc. I am an LPC, and I have worked in this field in many capacities for approximately-17+ years in Missouri. The short version is I have worked in the field of residential care for children and adolescents with behavior disorders, domestic violence, in-patient psych, out-patient psych, and now private practice. I've been in private practice for 10 years. If you really want my full résumé, please e-mail me at tara@taralpc.com. I'll send it to you.

I come from a pretty funny family. Not the "knock knock who's there" kind but the witty, sarcastic, prank-pulling kind of family. Add in that I'm the youngest of my family and somehow that equaled I was the family clown, center of attention, the kid that got away with everything- according to my brother and sister. Here I am, that person that finds something funny in almost any situation. Did you ever see National Lampoon's Vacation movie? Remember where they tied the dog to the bumper and forgot him and drove off? I laughed until I almost peed my pants. (Please know I adore animals. At this moment we have two cats, a dog, and a horse. They are all rescues of one way or another.) My Dad found that scene funny too. My Mom thought we were sick in the head.

My ability to find humor in most situations sometimes makes people uncomfortable. One of my graduate professors told me my laughter was a sign of nervousness and that I had to stop laughing in my sessions. That statement got stuck inside my head like a fishhook gets stuck in your skin. You know you just can't get it out without doing more damage. The statement kind of festered, got mentally infected, and I started wondering if something was seriously wrong with me. No matter what I did, I just kept laughing. In sessions, out of sessions, you name it - laughter follows me wherever I go.

My co-workers always asked how I seemed to have my clients laughing so much. My clients were notorious for telling me jokes. I've just never found a way to stop having fun in my sessions. I married a funny guy. He's so funny he makes me mad because if we are in a discussion (and of course I'm right but he's trying to prove me wrong), he will find a way to make me laugh. I do the same thing to him though. I have friends who call me during life crises just so I can make them laugh and help them alleviate their stress. I have this theory that we all have at least one superpower; sometimes we have more, but for sure we have at least one.

Humor is one of my superpowers. My other superpower is the ability to piss people off. I'll write a book about that later. Here I am, a Licensed Professional Counselor in Missouri with the superpower of laughter. What do I do with that you ask? I treat survivors of trauma, particularly survivors of sexual violence, veterans with PTSD, as well as survivors of childhood abuse, grief, domestic violence, and other traumatizing events And I help them overcome all those emotional pain points with humor. Yes humor. Honestly, laughter really is the best medicine. It's free. It has only a few side effects- sore tummy muscles and for some it makes them pee a bit. If you aren't sure about this laughter stuff, just take a moment and read the side effects of any psychiatric medication…scary. I once took a medication for a sinus infection that had a rare tropical disease listed as a side effect. I live in Missouri. How was I going to get a rare tropical disease from a medication?? I am in NO WAY saying to have your clients stop their medications!!

Think about this: How do you feel after a session with a client? Do you feel alive and excited or drained and burnt out? When they come back next week can you predict what they are going to talk about? Have you experienced secondary trauma from just hearing about what your clients have been through? Truthfully, I don't. Not any more. It's time to get more laughter in your sessions and your life. Life is far too short so have some fun. Yes, I know you were taught that therapy is serious work and that we need to respect our clients' feelings. There is another way to conduct sessions that is respectful and fun; and it's also effective at clearing the client's painful emotions while it eliminates your burnout. Sessions really can be fun, healing, and transformative.

Lastly just a quick note. I have several references of books, articles, and the like for further reading in the back of this book. In an effort to keep this book fun and helpful I've refrained from citing everything and anything. I'm aiming for this to be a fun, short, and inspiring book.

Chapter 1
Giggle, Snort- Where Are We Going On This Trip?

"Common sense and a sense of humor are the same thing, moving at different speeds. A sense of humor is just common sense dancing."- William James

As I mentioned before, it is my intention to make this book as short and sweet as possible. First, who has time to read a long, long book? We are drowning in a sea of information from TV, newspapers, books, journal articles, and social media. Second, I can't stand books that have lots of extra fluff just to make them long and "professional."

In a research done by Webster and Hackett, approximately 54% of mental health professionals in Northern California reported high emotional exhaustion. I know the majority of my friends in the field have reported burnout. Some have left the field entirely, some have changed jobs frequently, and others just keep on keeping on. Basically there is a high burnout rate in this field. We all got into this field for one reason or another. I have not been immune to this burnout. After about 3 years of working in a community based psychiatric facility, I was so burnt out I'm sure I smelled like charcoal all day. I tried and tried to get a new job in the field and out of the field. I was turned down by many places within this field and was turned down by every place outside this field. I eventually applied to go back to school to become a chiropractor and was actually accepted. Long story short, I opted to buy a house and stay in the field versus going further into student loan debt.

Honestly I kind of fell into this field. I took a psychology class while majoring in horses. I found it very interesting, and I realized that working in the horse industry was not going to be a good fit for me. I love horses but when I take jobs working with them I lose my passion for them. Horses have made sense to me since forever. People never did. This psychology class was helping me understand humans. In turn I added psychology as a second major in undergrad. This was a subject that fascinated me, and as long as I'm interested and having fun I though I might as well see what a career in psychology would be like. So I slapped a second major on to my college career.

Now take a moment. Get out a piece of paper and pen and take the time to write out honest answers to the following questions:

Why did you get into this field?

What did you think this career was really going to be like?

What do you enjoy about it?

What have you really disliked about it?

How do you want it to be, look, feel?

When I started on my graduate degree, I was told that this field was a thankless and financially fruitless job. But I kept powering on. In fact I was taught that essentially humans are damaged, broken, and will be so forever with only a few minor improvements. (Yes, welcome to my graduate training!) When I got into the full-fledged real world working in community psych, I was further taught how doing anything was not going to really be helpful. I had already had the mindset of empowerment versus enabling.

My places of employment kept telling me I had to keep my clients coming back. That translates to me as secretly saying "keep them sick so they keep coming, so the company makes money."

Lots of burn out. Lots of it. Everywhere I turn. Even today. I have family and friends in this field still chugging along and still looking to get out. What happened to the reason they got into this field? Was there ever a passion for it? For some, no. For others yes, but that passion has been dampened. Let's just reignite that flame, shall we? I'm thinking you are looking to reignite your love of the work you do! I'm assuming that's what you're looking for or you wouldn't have picked this book.! I'm 100% about helping you love what you do!

Here's what I see is part of the problem: clients aren't getting better or they are but it's just tiny bits of improvement then possibly back sliding. In working in an environment like that, it becomes depressing. Hearing the same complaint or story week in and week out. Trying to stay present and follow your clients' emotions. Helping them feel their feelings as I like to say. How about we just take a dramatic path change and come at this from a completely different angle? Humor, laughter, and smiles. Think about when you smile at someone, Don't you feel slightly better yourself? And then don't they start to feel a tad bit better also? This is the domino, pay it forward effect, and it is actually possible through humor. Laughter is truly a great medicine. When we lighten up, our clients lighten up and their minds start to update and change.

In the following chapters, we will get into the inner workings of the human emotional mind, the times that humor isn't helpful, how to incorporate humor, and, lastly, where else to go to further your knowledge and experience with this idea of therapeutic humor.

As we begin chapter 2, let's look at this whole thing from a different perspective. I will be brutally honest here: being naturally funny is very helpful and makes this easier. If you are naturally funny, then you will have an innate understanding of why and how to use humor more effectively. If you've sensed you've lost your funny bone then let's intend to find it again! And if you've just never been funny let's see where that funny bone is hiding. Lastly, if you detest funny and laughter- put this book down and read something else. My feelings won't be hurt at all!

Chapter 2
Reasons Why You Should Be Funny In A Session

"Kindness and a generous spirit go a long way. And a sense of humor. It's like medicine- very healing."- Max Irons

I think it would be best for me to clarify that this is a whole new and, for some, different way to look at the human mind. I know it is radically different than what I was taught in graduate school as I mentioned before. It really is amazing I even finished with my degree. I'm going to make a big leap here and 1) assume you are still reading this and 2) that you are looking to find something new, different, and helpful. You probably wouldn't have picked up this book otherwise.

Now as a yogi might say- "Clear your mind." That's your homework assignment right now. For a little while, set aside everything you have been taught and everything you have learned, and just see this as it is - a suggestion to how the mind works. (Some is based upon research while some is just my professional and personal opinion. I will do my best to let you know which is research and which is Tara-talk.) Lastly, shelf your clients, current or past. This way of thinking gets cumbersome if you are trying to learn it and apply it to clients at the same time.

First let me give credit where credit is due. This whole concept and perspective of how the mind works came from Dr. Jon Connelly, Ph.D, LCSW. He is the creator and founder of The Institute of Rapid Resolution Therapy® (IRRT). Then, Courtney Armstrong, LPC helped me understand the actual "whys" on why we do things this way and how neuroscience plays into this concept of laughter as the best medicine. At the end of this book, I will provide you links and information on how to train with both Dr. Connelly and Courtney, which I highly recommend. I also want to note that this is a simplistic way of looking at how the human mind works. We all know the brain is a very, very complicated organ. I'm notorious for taking the simple and making it harder than it needs to be as well as taking the complex and making it simple.

It has been said that on conscious versus subconscious mind, conscious mind is 5% of our mind and subconscious mind is 95% of our mind. How about we start with getting a better understanding of subconscious mind? (If you'd like to know more about this detail, read "The Biology of Belief by Dr. Bruce H. Lipton, Ph.D.)

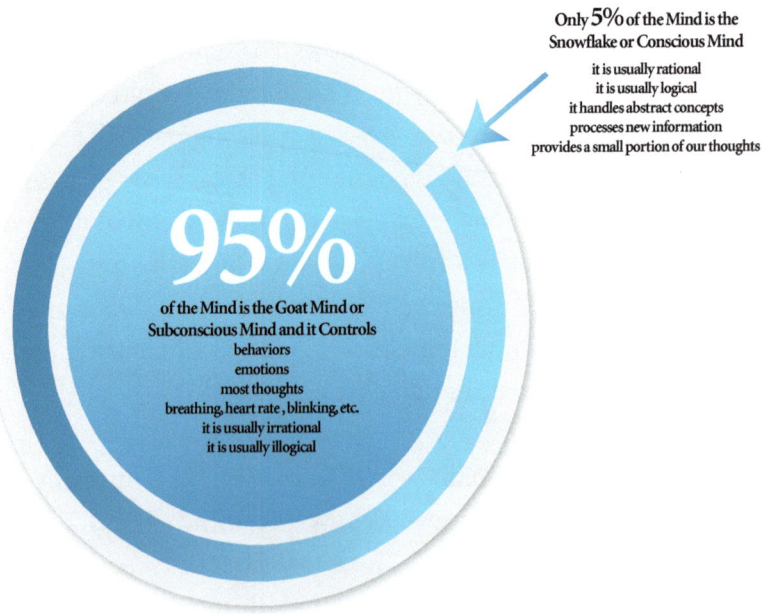

Only **5%** of the Mind is the Snowflake or Conscious Mind

it is usually rational
it is usually logical
it handles abstract concepts
processes new information
provides a small portion of our thoughts

95%
of the Mind is the Goat Mind or Subconscious Mind and it Controls
behaviors
emotions
most thoughts
breathing, heart rate, blinking, etc.
it is usually irrational
it is usually illogical

Subconscious mind is the multitasker of our mind. It manages our breathing, heart rate, blinking, emotions, behaviors, and most of our thoughts. It likely manages about 80-90% of our thoughts. I haven't found any research on that, it's just from my experience that I came up with that percentage. Basically it can do a million things indefinitely. Any task that we do regularly our subconscious mind takes over. I like to think that when athletes and artists are "in the zone" their subconscious mind has taken over and is doing the work for them. I know from being in sessions with clients that sometimes I say and do things that I've not really put a lot of energy and conscious effort into. I'm pretty sure my subconscious mind has just flown me through sessions and gotten me to say just the right thing at just the right time. The interesting thing to note about our subconscious mind is it functions at about the level of a goat. I told you this was a new and different way of thinking about our minds!

The other 5% is conscious mind. It is <u>not</u> a multitasker. It does one thing for a short amount of time. Remember studying for your licensure exam and you got brain fried? Yep, that's your conscious mind running out of steam. So when we learn something, it first starts in our conscious mind and then transfers into our subconscious mind. Our conscious mind is the only part of our mind that understands abstract concepts. The biggest, most widely used abstract concept is Time. Past. Present. Future. And the time on your clock, well your smart phone, actually. Think about it, goats don't actually keep track of time. They just keep track of urges- hunger, sex, sleep, etc. Conscious mind is the rational and logical part of our mind. It's pretty small compared to "goat" mind. So small let's liken it to being the size of a snowflake. One tiny snowflake. (I have Dr. Jon Connelly, Ph.D to thank for this outlook and it works very well for me and my clients. Again it's just a way of looking at conscious versus subconscious mind.)

Separate goat mind and snowflake work great. But goat and snowflake basically speak different languages. Therefore together things can get complicated. It's like things get lost in translation.

Conscious or
Subconscious?

I'm certain that our human minds are more complicated than a computer or car. Anything complicated needs tune ups and updates. Thus our human minds can greatly benefit from a tune up or update. This is something that I take full responsibility to do in my sessions. That's not all though. We experience trauma in our lives. Sometimes it's large trauma like sexual violence or veterans; sometimes it's a small trauma like having to put your nose in the corner in third grade. Either way, trauma has an impact on our subconscious mind. Within our goat mind, trauma creates a small domino effect of other problematic things.

First, our goat mind confuses the impression of the thing (the memory of what happened) with what actually happened. Thus a client may have been molested 20 years ago, but her emotional mind reacts exactly the same to that memory as it did when it happened. Second, our mind adds meaning to the thing that happened and the meaning is distorted and 100% worse than what actually happened. For example, survivors of sexual violence usually come in with the following meanings attached to themselves: "I'm damaged goods; everyone can tell I was molested when I was five years old; I'm so stupid for letting that happen to me." These are pretty drastic meanings for something that happened 20 years ago. And honestly I don't believe one of those meanings. Yet meanings always get added to traumatic events. Another way of thinking of meanings is that they are the negative tape, with all those painful, hurtful, critical thoughts, that's played inside the person's head.

Third, our mind scans our personal history, sorts through our memories, and can also scan our potential future for situations that have similarity and confuse them as being the same. Think about a friend who calls you up after a bad day at work. She/he tells you about what happened at work and then 30 minutes later you're hearing how something that happened to her/him in high school is the same thing as what happened today. Similar=Same. Then a facet of the subconscious mind gathers all that up- meanings and similar experiences-piles it all on a turkey platter and gets lost and thinks that turkey platter is the only thing happening- ever. Please note that this is just a facet of our goat mind; there's still the majority of it doing what it needs to do to keep us alive and functioning.

As I said earlier, our goat mind is responsible for our emotions, including the good ones and the not so great ones too. Let's just focus on the not so great ones: sadness, anxiety, anger, guilt, and grief. (And the many faces of each of those emotions.) These problematic emotions are designed for one reason and one reason only: To motivate us to get something in the world to stop. When something traumatic happens, our subconscious mind creates a painful emotion to motivate us to get something to stop from happening. That's it. That's all emotions are about. (Reminder: I said this was a different way of looking at this.) I have no respect for painful feelings. What so ever. I have no empathy for problematic emotions. When a client walks in my door oozing some painful emotion, I kick into high gear to eradicate that emotion and update my client's subconscious mind. I'm gearing to get their emotions in a much better place.

These emotions have specific drives in mind, yet our society doesn't allow for the reaction we are designed to have according to our goat mind.

 **ANGER**

Move forward and bite the thing threatening us.

 **ANXIETY**

Run away from the thing threatening us.

 **SADNESS**

Change the past. *(this is different in the case of clinical depression)*

 **GRIEF**

Stop someone or something from dying.

 **GUILT**

Make one feel like shit now so they
will behave better in the past.

(This is a different way of looking at emotions. Just try this hat on with me for a while.)

Another way of thinking about this is that when we experience something traumatic we automatically and sometimes unknowingly get an app downloaded that has a virus in it. Eventually that virus begins to affect other areas of our mind and thus our life. As humans, we have the ability to recall information, times, and places unlike any other animal on the planet. In doing so, because our subconscious mind is so primitive, it then thinks that the event is happening RIGHT NOW. Therefore it creates an emotion to motivate us to stop that event from happening. The truth is none of us has a time machine to go back in time to change what happened. (If you do have a time machine, please don't tell me because I fear it will mess up my business; but I'm not sure if it will better my business or bring it to a close, so I'd rather just not know.) This leaves us with many clients who have painful emotions happening about things that they really have no ability to change.

How do we help them then? Humor. Why humor? Because two opposing emotions cannot exist at the same time over one event. Humor and laughter is like shining a light into a dark room. Darkness cannot exist with light. Let me repeat this again- Two opposing emotions cannot exist at the same time about a traumatic event. Honestly though, laughter is a lot more fun than continuing to cry or vent about something. It's a regular occurrence that my clients, while in session, are laughing about what they went through. Many of my clients aren't sure that what happened in the session, going from crying to laughter, will last. Apparently they think the walls of my office are magical. Yet weeks, months, and years later they contact me saying how they are still noticing the positive effects of their session. I think one of the biggest benefits about using laughter as a therapeutic tool is that it's something different and unusual and it's very likely clients are not expecting to laugh in a session.

There is research out there suggesting that the way to integrate a traumatic event is to talk about it while staying emotionally present. (For more information on this, read Unlocking the Emotional Brain by Bruce Ecker et al.) Why not take that a step further and get their emotional mind to find some fun and laughter while telling the story? In doing so, the emotional mind sees no reason to continue to create problematic emotions about that event. Something can't be scary if we are laughing about it, or so goat mind thinks!

Back when I first began to write this book, my neighbor and friend dropped by after work. She stated she'd had a really bad day. I made us each a martini and said "Tell me about your day and I'll tell you about mine. Then we shall see who wins the shittiest day contest." She immediately said she didn't want to tell me and so I insisted. Well that very day she had been officially diagnosed with breast cancer. So she won the contest fair and square. We proceeded for several hours to chat and find the humor in this really tough situation. What's funny about breast cancer you ask? Well for one now her medical health would be far worse than everyone else. She was already using her diagnosis to get out of cleaning the kitty litter boxes and taking out trash. I asked if she would get a handicap parking sticker and if I could get one too just to support her. Lastly she was going to get breast implants when all this was said and done. As a woman who has been flat chested my whole life I thought that was a huge bonus to this crap situation. And seriously she has been free and clear for about a year now and her boobs look great! That night laughter lightened the load. Throughout her treatment we found time to stop, connect, and laugh. Humor may not have cured her but it did make her journey to wellness much easier.

Back to our topic here. Goat mind is creating emotions to motivate people to change or stop something from happening in the past and even possibly in the future. When we get the emotional mind to shift its emotional reaction to something, then the behaviors will also stop. One thing that tends to fuel those emotions and behaviors are "should, could, and would" statements. I believe those come from our snowflake/conscious mind. If you've ever worked with a goat or goats you likely know one tiny snowflake isn't very likely to make a goat do anything. So one should, could, or would statement isn't likely to change one's behaviors. And how many clients come in with "could, would, should" statements? This means we need to adjust their emotions. Those emotions are created by subconscious mind and therefore we will work with subconscious mind the way it works. Conscious mind understands abstract ideas. Subconscious mind is responsive to stories, metaphors, and symbols. Working humorously with stories, metaphors and symbols we can shift their emotional mind so it's working to their best benefit. Therefore they emotionally heal faster, our sessions are more fun, and we enjoy our work more. Remember how I noted earlier that subconscious and conscious mind speak different languages? Well here's a breakdown of each one's "language."

**Subconscious/
Goat Mind:**

**Symbols
Metaphors
Stories**

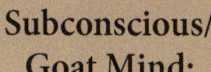

**Conscious/
Snowflake Mind**

**Abstract
Philosophical**

Chapter 3:
That's Just Not Funny- A Cautionary Tale For When Laughter May Not Be The Best Medicine

"The problem with having a sense of humor is often that people you use it on aren't in a good mood.."-
Lou Holtz

Laughter is not the answer for everyone and every situation. For sure humor and laughter will not be effective for those clients who lack any funny bone in them at all. And those clients do exist. I usually see it in those who work in Information Technology and engineers. You know that you know someone personally or professionally who just doesn't have an ounce of funny in them, which is different than those who just can't tell a funny joke to save their life but really are funny and fun to be around. So if you're dealing with a client who's just not funny or doesn't like fun this isn't the path to take with them.

There are a few other reasons, situations, and times that holding off on humor is a good idea. First and foremost is if the client just isn't ready to be OK. For instance, they just really aren't ready to be done with anxiety. My graduate program referred to this as a resistant client. I really don't see it as resistance any more. It is because there is a bigger payoff for having these problems than there is for being healthier. My suggestion- Ask them if it's OK to be OK. Sometimes you have to get detailed and microscopic about that question. For example, would it be OK to no longer have anxiety? I'll bet ya they say "Yes." Then ask what wouldn't be OK about that. You may get some really interesting answers. One answer I got to that very question was that if she (my client) was healthy no one would pay attention to her and therefore no one would love her, and then she'd be all alone. WHOA!!! I didn't see that one coming. This usually means I have to figure out how to get them on my side of the fence where being healthier emotionally and physically is way better than being ill. To be frank here, doing that requires being manipulative. I can come at them with science on how the mind works, or how being healthier improves their relationships versus makes them lose relationships. I like to think of myself as a Jedi Knight from Star Wars. I use the Force (manipulation) for good not evil. It's always aimed at the best interest of the client. Sounds crazy and to some even horrible, but I'm just being honest here. I'm a natural born story-teller so I can whip up a story to help them understand how great it would be to jump the fence into the land of healthier than stay on the side of emotional stagnation.

Not every client comes in with a conflict like that. Some, if they could have, would have boxed up all their problematic emotions and gifted them to me. Those clients make it easy peasy for me. Some clients are really gung-ho about getting better until we really start to get to work. Then we have to fret through minor details of the possible benefits to being emotionally unhealthy. Again I go back to using the Force. There's an element of this that requires being able to really roll with the punches as it's been said - to zig and zag and yet keep them and the session moving forward. The more you do this, the more success you will have and the more energy you will naturally have to continue to zig and zag. As I write this, I can see how this may sound very draining. It's really not. As you stay present and focused this becomes effortless.

Grief is the first problematic emotion that is most likely not going to respond well to humor and laughter. Grief is an emotional response to a loss, usually of a loved one, but I've had clients who came in grieving the loss of a job. This is one emotion that many times people aren't ready to be free of. And to be willing to free them of this emotion it's helpful to see and understand that this emotion is not helping our clients. You may not agree with me on this one. Some people really believe (therapists and clients alike) that they need to feel and experience grief. I can see and understand this to a point and at that point, which is different for different people, it becomes problematic and dysfunctional. Once it becomes problematic the slide into dysfunctional is quick, and it only gets more dysfunctional the longer the grief is there. So if you are reading this and you really believe that it's OK for someone to live in grief for decades you might want to just skip this section. I'm not here to argue my point. Because the bottom line is if problematic emotions didn't become dysfunctional we'd likely not be in business.

There is, however, the idea held by many in our society that grief is necessary. Clients may think that if they are no longer grieving then they are not honoring those that they lost. Give or take your beliefs of what happens after death, my thought here is those we lost really aren't looking for us to be miserable in grief. But this grief thing goes beyond that. Family members will influence one's grief. I knew an RRT therapist who worked week after week on a client's grief; she'd be better after a session, go home, and come back the next week back in deep miserable grief. This therapist consulted with me repeatedly and I asked over and over had the client agreed that not grieving would be best. The answer was always yes. What was throwing a wrench in the gears is the client would go visit her mother in between sessions and, when she was doing better and not so stuck in grief, her mother found ways to make her feel grief deeply and painfully. Her mom felt everyone needed to grieve this loss forever; Mom was very much of the mindset that being emotionally ill was a good thing.

People's religious views can also influence their ability and willingness to move beyond grief. Another therapist who had consulted with me had a client whose son had committed suicide. According to her religious background, her son was burning in hell, and she was not willing to look at this situation from any other angle. The thought of her son burning in hell was terrifying to her and thus this therapeutic relationship was ended because of her unwillingness to move forward. (Now the idea of ending treatment with clients is one for another book which I shall leave to someone else to write.) Grief is the number one issue my office manager and I try to screen before the client even gets to my office. We ask very frankly "is it OK to be free of this grief?" "Are you ready to walk away from this pain and forward into a healthier life?" Currently a lot of the clients that I see for grief have been referred to me by other clients who have had successful grief- relieving sessions. Those referrals have seen the changes in my previous clients and they call because they want to receive the treatment that will result in the same changes in themselves. So not as much screening is necessary.

Now maybe the clients have other things that are bothersome to them but aren't ready to move past the grief. Go for it, get that other stuff cleaned up. Likely they will see and feel the benefits and then they may be ready for a grief session. But also sometimes when a client is having difficulty with grief, humor isn't a great option. It's like their funny-bone has been lost. That's OK. You can take some of the suggestions discussed in the next chapter and adjust and adapt them to be less funny I don't find the loss of someone's loved one funny. It's not funny, and we all know that. You will have to use your experience and gut instincts on this. I trust you will handle it the best way possible for your client(s).

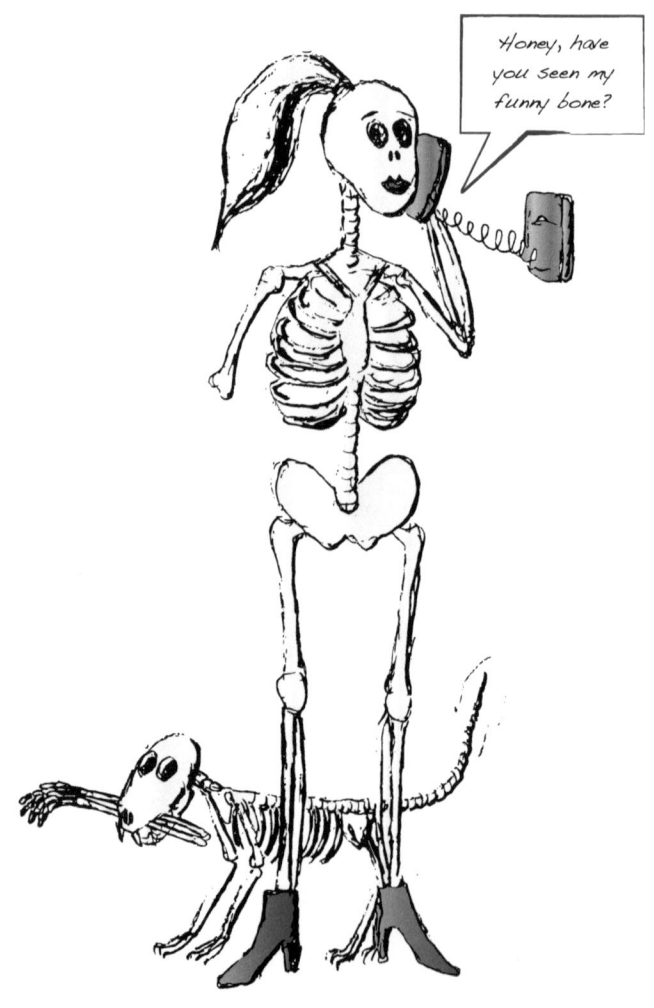

Now the next most challenging emotion I find to get clients cleared of is guilt and this is pretty much for very similar reasons as grief. People really think they need and must have guilt. We are taught that guilt makes us better humans. People have fear that without guilt they will be consciously meanies. Guilt fuels and feeds other problematic emotions that then create other unwanted behaviors. I believe without guilt we are wiser and have more clarity, which leads us to being more rational and logical.

The second problematic emotion that may not respond well to humor is anger of any form. I see more anger in men than women but it affects both. Sometimes people are not OK being free from anger. What I've realized is that they think they have power with anger and that the other person deserves their anger. Consequently, they think that by being angry they are punishing that person. Ever heard the cliché' "Anger is like drinking the poison and expecting the other person to die?" Same for resentment, jealousy, etc. When someone comes in with anger as their default emotion it sometimes can take time to get to the point of using humor to diffuse it. As long as they are good with being done with the anger you will be able to do so. Many clients with anger really initially need someone to just hear and understand their side of the story. Patience is usually the key here. If the bottom line is they really want to keep the anger, laughter isn't going to work. No matter what, it's still their life. I have had a few clients that no matter how I tried to explain how they would benefit from being free of the anger they still weren't ready to be healthier. Even being a manipulative storyteller sometimes doesn't get me the results I'm looking for. We win some we lose some.

What about clients with depression you ask? I see depression as coming in a few different ways. There's sadness, blues type thing. This is easily remedied with humor. I also think there's situational depression. Something that is happening or has happened has triggered the sadness. Usually the sadness is about not being able to change something they have no ability to change. Or they are so freaking mad about the situation the mind's emotional response has slipped into sadness or depression. All of these can respond well to laughter and humor.

Then of course there's clinical depression. This is a whole different beast to me. Laughter and humor will fall flat as a pancake when facing someone with clinical depression. Maybe it's the years of working with chronically mentally ill adults, but usually it's within a few minutes on the phone or in person that I can sense that clinical depression. Something happens with clinical depression that locks the emotional mind up and humor will not only fall flat I had it, once, blow up in my face. The client came in presenting extremely angry. She had survived a horrific trauma years prior and was emotionally and actually physically haunted by it. I was zigging and zagging for like 2 hours trying to get the full OK to clear this trauma and at the start of hour 3 the clinical depression finally showed up. Sadly her psychiatrist had never put her on antidepressants despite her request for them. Amazingly enough this client was totally wanting a new psychiatrist, so I made that happen for her and saw her a few times after that to give her a therapeutic base to get through the medication changes. Once on her new meds she did much, much better. She has yet to want to get her trauma cleared. I'm just grateful she fell into my hands so she could get on medications more effective for her.

Clinical depression seems to have some shrinkage effects on the hippocampus. The hippocampus apparently plays a big part in memory. And there seems to be some issue with a dysfunctional amygdala and depression. Maybe clinical depression is so challenging to treat with laughter because of all that. Honestly I just don't know for sure other than something seems locked up and hard to move with just laughter. I have heard that actual physical movement is beginning to show positives signs of alleviating severe depression. Maybe I need to incorporate dance into my sessions!?

Lastly, chronic mental illness of any sort again seems to have little response to humor. That's not to say someone with Bipolar who is stable when on their meds cannot benefit from some laughter, but surely you know someone with chronic mental illness. You can imagine (yes I know I told you to shelf your clients, just flow with me here) someone you know with a severe mental illness and imagine trying to get them to laugh about something they went through. If someone is dealing with hallucinations, paranoia, and delusions I doubt I have to tell you but I will anyway- avoid humor and laughter. I had a client once who was in his late teens with some form of Autism or Asperger's who had hallucinations. My style of humor and such was not helpful to him. Nor was his father happy to hear I agreed with his son's diagnosis and highly suggested medications. (That's one way to get fired- advocate for your client to get care that the client's family doesn't feel is necessary.)

Maybe the big picture of chronic mental illness falls into that whole amygdala and hippocampus thing. I really just don't fully know for sure. I just know someone who has a severe mental illness has a difficult time accepting humor and laughter as a way to alleviate and reduce any problematic emotions. As I said earlier, I want to be as helpful as possible in a book. I find it helpful when I learn new things to know what situations this new skill might not be suited for.

Chapter 4:
The Funny Pages- How To Bring Laughter Into Your Sessions

"Humor has bailed me out of more tight situations than I can think of. If you go with your instincts and keep your humor, creativity flows. With luck, success comes, too."- Jimmy Buffett

Finally, the chapter you've been waiting for - how to incorporate laughter. I'm going to remind you again, two opposing emotions cannot exist at the same time about a traumatic event. First things first: we must get the person's attention emotionally and mentally to the present moment. I'm talking about our client(s) but really us as well. Many people, when thinking or talking about something traumatic, become emotionally hypnotized by the situation. They feel those feelings as though it's happening right now. The majority of my clients have survived really tragic traumas. When they come in and tell me about those events they become emotional, start crying, or even withdraw from me and the session. I know you've seen clients do all of those before. Lesson one- get them present with you! And stay present yourself. What happened to them is done and over with, it's not happening right now. Unless you do some odd therapy practice I've never heard of, I doubt you are throwing live hand grenades at them. Where they are is safe. They made it to your office therefore by golly let's get excited that they made it through those traumatic events and to you!

How do we get them and keep present? We go back to the research that suggests the way the brain integrates trauma is talking about the traumatic event while staying emotionally present. In other words the brain re-wires itself from painful emotions about what has happened to being emotionally neutral about that situation that's no longer happening. I know we've all spent tons of time with clients encouraging them to cry, to go with the feeling, to feel it more, feel it deeper, just BE that emotion. Well no more I say, no more! The first thing I let my clients know when they get to the point of where they are going to tell me in detail about what happened is that we are going to talk about it while staying emotionally present. For many I explain the neuroscience behind why to stay emotionally present. It's about intention. We intend to both stay emotionally present while telling this story, this small facet of their life. By the sheer fact we both intended it, it's more likely to happen. By them understanding how the mind works- the whole goat mind versus snowflake it has set them up to be better able to stay present while telling their story. Even being educated like that about their mind is different. And I do tell them it's my job to get their trauma cleared. That, for 99% of them, is new and very exciting.

Now I know, I know - aren't we supposed to be all client centered and collaborate on an agreed treatment plan? Yes and no. If you are a provider of insurance you will have to do the required treatment plans. If you don't take insurance I'm sure you already collaborate with your clients on what the agreed goals and targets are. I am not an insurance provider so I do a lot of collaborating with my clients. Therefore we agree on what's been problematic, and I figure out what the target is for them; how I intend for them to feel and respond after our session. Yes, I discuss this with them. Yes, they can change, add, or delete parts or the whole darn thing and I start over. Once we get one that we both agree upon then that's where we aim the session. So yes, it's client centered but therapist driven. It's kind of like I'm the emotional mechanic and it's my job to get their emotional brain tuned up and repaired. If they could have fixed it prior to their session they would have.

Clients are relieved to find out it's my job not theirs. So now we have this target that we are aiming for as well as the intention to remain emotionally present while reviewing any traumatic event they may have dealt with. That's a great start already to our clients being healthier afterwards and us being less burnt out. The next step is to help them narrow the event to be updated down to a very specific one, time, place etc. For example, some clients come in with five years of being molested. We are looking for just one of those many times. Maybe it's the first time they were molested; maybe it's the time that haunts them most. Specifics and details are needed, not generalities. Details can be anything- where, when, what clothes was everyone wearing, how was the room decorated, what season or time of year was it, how did they feel, what did they do? Why details and specifics? Because that's what our subconscious mind is responsive to; it understands details; it doesn't understand generalities.

It's common, as you already know, for clients to get emotional while telling their tales. When this happens it's our job to 1) stay present ourselves and 2) help them stay present because even when we both intend to be present emotions slip. There are several ways to help them stay present. One thing I do a lot is interrupt them and ask for really irrelevant details- time of year, what month, what day of the week, what picture in the room do they like, what's their dog's name, what did they have for dinner last night, even what color shoes I have on. Once that question didn't work so well, apparently my client was color blind. He then proceeded to tell me how his wife color coordinates his closet and labels green shirts and brown shirts. It did end up getting him present and he was able to continue with his story with much less emotional charge. The thing is just ask them something that basically snaps them out of their emotional mind and back with you, as long as those questions are ethical and legal…not that I really have to say that but just in case.

You can also stop them and have them give you a command kind of like Simon says. So tell them to have you do something with your arms and they will say something like "touch your left index finger to your nose" and you have to hold that till the next interruption to tell you something else. One- this interrupts their emotional charge. Two- it gives them a sense of control, and three - you will look silly which is kind of the whole point of this book! Laughter and humor.

You can build them up throughout their story telling by encouraging any details they note. So if they say "well it was fall around Thanksgiving…" you say "Oh wow GREAT detail, good job." And just interject throughout the story telling phase with positive reinforcement. Similar to the other suggestions, it keeps them present and it also builds up their sense of pride and accomplishment.

Other therapists I know use tapping. If you have an EFT (Emotional Freedom Technique) certification this will likely help you and your clients even more than this short explanation (but it's not necessary to be EFT certified to use a tap here and there to shift the emotional focus.) I suggest starting by asking them if you can tap their hand or knee with a pencil gently. If they say yes, demonstrate how you will tap and where. Ask if the tapping caused emotional distress- I doubt it did. Then during times they get emotional start tapping and ask them what they notice when you tapped them. To be honest, I prefer the theatrics and dramatics of getting them present. There have been times when I had to tap their arm or leg to get them present. When I've done so I look them in the eye and say "Hey come back here to me. How am I doing? Am I doing OK? Oh I am? Well then you must be doing OK too. Cause if I'm OK then you're OK." They laugh and we move on.

Let's move on to ways to get funny and laugh. This first suggestion is by far my favorite and the one I use the most. We start with the clients telling me their story, as we just discussed. Once they are done with the first round I tell them that I'm going to tell them their story and I'm going to get some parts right because I was listening and paying attention. When I get things right it is their job to say (like a snotty teenager or in some accent- client will laugh here usually) "FINALLY you got it RIGHT!!" And I tell them that I really do need them to let me know when I got it right because I like to receive positive reinforcement. (Client will again laugh.) I also inform them I will get some things wrong because 1) I wasn't actually there and 2) because sometimes I make a mistake. They in turn (with the snotty teenager voice or accent) must say "NO you're wrong…" and then correct what I messed up. Of course I get bits right but mostly I purposely mess things up royally and the messier and more crazy the change the better. Simple changes: change the time it happened, their age when it happened, where it happened. Dramatic changes-make everyone in their story wear scuba gear. Say that it happened in space. Tell the story as though everyone was singing the whole time. Get large and silly. For me this way appeals to my creative side, my joy of being on stage from when I was a kid.

Once I had a client who had some anxiety related issues that actually started due to some unknown medical issues and then turned into full blown anxiety issues. One day, prior to knowing about the medical issues, she and her children went to church. She began to feel emotionally upset and had to leave church. Unfortunately for her but fortunately for me, that day the church was packed and she and the kids had to sit right in front. When she and the kids left, she had to pass everyone by to get outside and home. She spent years thinking everyone in church had judged her and criticized her behind her back for leaving.

As she told me this story I had a great idea to make the story light, funny, and slap-sticky. I had her picture the event and then retold the story. First go round she left because she was having major flatulence problems (something she would die of embarrassment from and she started to tell me how that's not what happened. I stated I knew that but to watch my version of the movie.). I had her watch the movie again where as she left she waved bye to everyone and stated things like "My kid just pooped his pants, I just started my period, I have terrible hiccups, etc. etc." I told the story as though she and the kids walked down the aisle waving like the British monarchy. In one version she and the kids skipped down the aisle singing and such. I kept telling and retelling this tale until finally she looked at me and said "I bet they were all actually jealous and wanted to go home too." This incident had been recorded as the start to her anxiety and panic attacks. Once her mind saw it in a new light, her mind's emotional reaction to it completely changed. Bear in mind this was not one of my easier sessions. We still got there in the end.

Another way to laugh up clients' stories is ask them to just give you a newspaper headline snapshot of what happened to them. Don't even get the whole gory detailed story. Then do as I noted above, tell their story back to them in great detail, obviously with literal mistakes due to not knowing anything about their story. You will likely still get some things correct because I bet someone else had a similar story. Throughout, they have to interrupt you and tell you when you are right; when I get it right from this way I get all excited about being right more so than when they told me their full story. And they interrupt me when I get it wrong and again they correct the information. I then go back and restate the story with the correct information. It's like taping and re-taping over an old VCR tape, eventually it just won't tape anything anymore.

You can also have them tell their entire story, details and all, with some odd accent- British, robot, Valley girl. In doing so, they are keeping their emotional mind focused on the present versus getting emotional over the past. When using accents, I think it's best to aim for the weirdest, most challenging accents possible. Maybe even you use an accent while encouraging them, interrupting them, and asking questions. Believe me, neither of you will be able to keep a straight face unless one of you was, or is, a full time paid actor.

Probably my second favorite way to clear trauma is this: First I explain to them that the words "I can't!" are very powerful. It's common for someone to reevaluate a past event and come up with numerous ways they could have or should have handled it. I know you've never done that yourself, but I bet clients have. When those ideas come up and we state clearly and assertively "I can't!" our emotional mind stops creating emotions about what had happened. So I have them practice the line "I can't" firmly, assertively, definitely, even aggressively. When we practice, I make suggestions such as "Go back this morning and don't brush your teeth." "Stop putting on that blouse today." Then I begin to filter in parts of their story. For example, the last story I told about the woman and her kids in church- "Stop going to church that day." "Move to another state three years before that all happened." OR say with someone who was abused as a child- "Go back and be born in Canada to a completely different family." "Hurry, join the circus before you ever were abused by so and so." The crazier and sillier, the better.

Sometimes clearing a trauma is just a matter of reframing it in a really ridiculous way. The following example is from another RRT therapist, Autumn Hahn,[1] based out of south Florida, who gave her permission to have this printed. (And she in fact blessed me with writing this section up

[1] Autumn Hahn is a Licensed Mental Health Counselor, Certified Clinical Hypnotherapist, and Certified Practitioner of Rapid Resolution Therapy® practicing at Clear Mind Group in South Florida .

herself.) Autumn was working with a female client whose husband had cheated on her. After telling the story of how the relationship ended, the woman stated that it was her fault that he had cheated on her; specifically, she said "I made him cheat on me." (FYI that statement is a meaning her mind attached to what happened.) Without blinking an eye, Autumn said, "That's the worst superpower ever." Of course the client was dumbfounded and said "What?" Autumn continued, "Everyone gets one superpower, right? You just have figured out what yours is. And yours is making men cheat on you? That's the worst superpower ever." The client laughed and, as the light went on in her mind, said, "No I didn't make him cheat on me. He chose to cheat. There was nothing I could have done to make him cheat or not cheat." Autumn returned with "Well good, now you've just got to figure out what your actual superpower is."

Once I had a previous client who had moved out of state contact me after his move. He asked for a phone session which is something I absolutely do not provide for initial appointments, but for some clients a phone call "tune up" is possible. A few days prior to his call he had been back in Missouri to finish up some things related to work. While taking a nap, the home he was staying in was broke into. When the burglar realized someone was home he began to physically assault my client. My client fought back and they tumbled down the stairs. Some way, somehow, the cops were contacted and the burglar was taken to jail. After this incident, my client was unable to sleep and was feeling anxious and fearful. After he finished with his story I asked him "Where you are now will a mountain lion eat you? Are you currently living in gang territory? Was this the scariest thing you've ever survived?" To the last question he stated

"Reframe it, write over it, and
find a way to make it light and funny."

no, he had survived a much scarier event many years ago. He informed me he had been an adult chaperone for a teen skiing trip and he was the driver. Upon returning home, the brakes went out on the bus. He controlled the bus's slide till he could head it into a snow bank and saved not only himself but 30 teens. Later that winter he took them on another ski trip just to make sure he felt safe doing so. My response? "Well look at that. You survived a bus accident, saved 30 teens, AND wrestled a burglar. Now go outside, go for a hike, and avoid being eaten by a mountain lion and stung by scorpions." (He was living in New Mexico at the time.) He laughed and laughed. It was all done. Seriously, the emotional connection to that event was done and over.

The entire point of this is take a traumatic story and retell it in a new and interesting way with a different emotional charge or no charge at all. Reframe it, write over it, and find a way to make it light and funny. I could spend hours and many, many pages filling this chapter with examples, but again who has the time to read a book that long?

In the end of all of this I'm always seeking for little gold nuggets that come from surviving traumatic events. For women who have survived sexual trauma and have children of their own, I discuss with them that as much as we don't like what happened to them that now as parents they have a better ability to protect their own children from such things. Or adults who were neglected or abused by their parents and they want to be better parents themselves, they now know how not to parent and are more likely to seek better ways to parent.

Here is one last little story of using humor to help move

people through and past trauma. This was with a friend of mine who's also a Licensed Professional Counselor and has trained in RRT. My friend's name is Kelly. This was during the time she was training in RRT, so we would attend the same trainings. At a few of these trainings, a fellow trainee, a male, developed a mild obsession about Kelly. This caused Kelly some emotional distress and it even brought forth some past issues regarding a guy from her past. I was trying to be a helpful friend and was trying different RRT methods to help her get the past and current issue cleared. Going to these trainings usually requires that we fly to another state and thus leave one of our cars at the park and fly places. These trainings are also long, 25 hours, three packed days of training. I tend to get home very brain fried and tired. We flew home after another long weekend of training with this guy who was obsessed with Kelly, and she's all upset about the situation. We are very, very jet lagged and slap happy by this time. We had been playing with the "I can't" process so I ended up just yelling at her various situations from her past and this recent thing, and she's responding in "I can't" until we both just fell out laughing so hard we may have peed our pants. Now for obvious reasons I don't recommend you yell at your clients. Shoot, this yelling therapy likely won't work with anyone but Kelly and I, but it was funny, then and now! Maybe using humor isn't the best form of counseling when you're seriously tired!

"I CAN'T!!!"

Chapter 5
The Last Laugh

"A sense of humor is...needed armor. Joy in one's heart and some laughter on one's lips is a sign that the person down deep has a pretty good grasp of life."- Hugh Sidey

The short and sweet of it is your private practice doesn't have to be stressful or draining. Ever seen the movie Rise of the Guardians? If you have, remember where Santa asks Jack Frost what's in his center? Later Jack Frost realizes his center is "fun." Well that's mine too. I do have the ability to find fun in many things that people don't find fun. Even cleaning house is fun; I turn on some music and get to work. (OK maybe I have some slight OCD about keeping a clean house, but it's only a smidge of OCD!) Just about anything I do with my horse is fun, even cleaning his stall. So it's significant to me personally to make my private practice fun. My dear friend Courtney Armstrong, LPC is doing trainings on creative play and fun in your practice to relieve burn out. I see the need for fun everywhere I turn in the mental health field. So often when talking to mental health professionals I hear so little enjoyment or fun in the work they do.

Currently I belong to a networking organization called Women's Power Networking. Locally we have a member who's a Certified Laughter Yoga Instructor. If you've never heard of this, it's someone who trained to make you laugh without you putting any effort into it. And no they are not stand-up comedians. The thing is I cannot sit next to this woman at networking events because she can make me laugh hysterically and, well, that interrupts the meetings we are having. I have attended a few of her laughter yoga sessions and you cannot stop her from getting you to laugh. It's truly infectious. If you're having trouble getting some laughter in your life, I highly suggest looking up laughter yoga and finding a session near you. Shoot, refer some clients who need some smiles and fun.

I won't lie to you; some clients really think counseling must be serious, intense, and painful. Some clients have sought other therapists because I no longer offer such sessions. Obviously clients find me; some even seek me out. When they do, they are quickly converted to this different way of counseling. Many of my clients then refer family or friends to me. Is there any better form of gratitude in this field than word of mouth referrals? Second to referrals are the e-mails and thank you cards I receive. Prior to packing my sessions with laughter and fun, I rarely got a thank you card or e-mail.

Take some time and think about what I have presented and suggested here. Play with some of the ideas and processes. Feel free, no I highly encourage you, to be creative with this idea and make it your own. Adjust it and shift it to fit your personality and your clients. There are stories I have used with clients that will only work for that specific client. That's perfectly OK!

This entire book was created just to inspire you to love your work and have fun with it. Being burnt out isn't helpful to you or your clients. What I have presented here certainly doesn't encompass everything I may do in a session or all the tidbits of stuff inside my professional mind. If it did I wouldn't have two more book ideas floating up inside my head. That aside, the humorous part of the work I do really is my most favorite piece.

It is my intention that this has been an easy, fun, and inspiring book for you. I have included a section of books to possibly read, trainings to possibly attend, references to refer to, and resources to possibly help you and your clients. With all that- Thank you, seriously. Thank you for purchasing this book and taking the time to read it. I never thought I'd ever actually get a book out there despite my desire to do so since high school, and now I have and you have taken time to spend with me! Much appreciation!

What's a pirate's favorite letter in the alphabet? Rrrrrrrr-
References, resources, recommended reading, research….

References and recommended reading:

Morse, Ph.D, G., Salyers, Ph.D, M. P., Rollins, Ph.D, A. L.,
Monroe-DeVita, Ph.D, M., & MSW, C. (n.d.). *Burnout in
Mental Health Services: A Review of the Problem and Its
Remediation.*

Lipton, B. H. (2008). *The Biology of Belief: Unleashing the
Power of Consciousness, Matter and Miracles.* N.p.: Hay
House.

Ecker, B., Ticic, R., & Hulley, L. (2012). *Unlocking the
Emotional Brain: Eliminating Symptoms at Their Roots
Using Memory Reconsolidation.* New York, NY: Routledge.

van der Kolk, B. A., McFarlane, A. C., & Weisaeth, M.
(1996). *Traumatic Stress: The Effects of Overwhelming
Experiences on Mind, Body, and Society.* New York, London:
Guilford Press.

Cozolino, L. (2010). *The Neuroscience of Psychotherapy:
Healing the Social Brain (2nd ed.).* New York, NY: W.W.
Norton & Company, Inc.

Ogden, P., Minton, K., & Pain, C. (2006). *Trauma and the
Body: A Sensorimotor Approach to Psychotherapy.* New
York, NY: W.W. Norton & Company, Inc.

Siegel, MD, D. J. (2010). *Mindsight: The New Science of
Personal Transformation.* New York, NY: Bantam Books.

Taylor, E. (2013). *Choices and Illusions: How Did I Get Where I Am, and How Do I Get Where I Want to Be?* Carlsbad, CA: Hay House.

Recommended reading authored by some of my Rapid Resolution Therapy friends:

Armstrong, LPC, C. (2015). *The Therapeutic "Aha!: 10 Strategies for Getting Your Client Unstuck.* N.p.: W.W. Norton & Company.

Armstrong, LPC, C. (2011). *Transforming Traumatic Grief: Six Steps to Move from Grief to Peace After the Sudden or Violent Death of a Loved One.* N.p.: Artemecia Press.

Chidley, LMHC, M. A. (2011). *Helping Hoarders: A Guide for Families, Counselors, and First Responders.* N.p.: Smashwords.

Richie-Melvan, Ph.D, S., & Vines, Ph.D, D. (2010). *Angel Walk: Nurses at War in Iraq and Afghanistan.* Portland, OR: Arnica Publishing, Inc.

Hahn, A. (2012). *Mini-Missions: Simplify and Add Joy to Your Life in Less Than 30 Minutes.* N.p.: CreateSpace Independent Publishing Platform.

Hahn, A. (2013). *Bubble Wrap Your Kids: A parenting Guide for preventio of childhood trauma.* N.p.: CreateSpace Independent Publishing Platform.

A few quick articles to read and inspire your funny side:

Smith, K. (2015, May 27). *No laughing matter? Counseling Today*. Retrieved July 22, 2015 from ct.counseling.org/2015/05/no-laughing-matter

Armstrong, LPC, C. (2013, July). *Creating Adventure and Play in Therapy: How to Vitalize Your Therapeutic Style*. Psychotherapy Networker. Retrieved July 8, 2014, from psychotherapynetworker.org/magazine/recentissues/2013-julaug/item/2157-creating-adventure-and-play-in-therapy/2157-creating-adventure-and-play-in-therapy

Madanes, C. (2014, May 5). *Finding Therapeutic Comedy in Tragedy: Mastering the Act of the Paradoxical Directive*. Psychotherapy Networker. Retrieved July 8, 2014, from daily.psychotherapynetworker.org/daily/professional-development/finding-therapeutic-comedy-in-tragedy/

Miller, L. (2014, January 1). *Editing Your Life's Stories Can Create Happier Endings. In Editing Your Life's Stories Can Create Happier Endings*. Retrieved July 8, 2014, from npr.org/blogs/health/2014/01/01/258674011/editing-your-lifes-stories-can-create-happier-endings

And a great TEDx video to watch:

Sutherland, R. (Writer). Sutherland, R. (Narrator). (2011). *Perspective is Everything* [Online video]. Athens: TEDxAthens. Retrieved July 8, 2014, from ted.com/talks/rory_sutherland_perspective_is_everything#t-17248

Resources

RAINN rainn.org

SAAM nsvrc.org/saam/sexual-assault-awareness-month-home

Jane Doe Advocacy Center janedoeadvocacy.wordpress.com/

Rapid Resolution Therapy rapidresolutiontherapy.com/

Laughter Yoga laughteryoga.org/english

Research on burnout

Burnout in Mental Health Services: A Review of the Problem and Its Remediation Gary Morse, Ph.D., Associate Executive Director, Michelle P. Salyers, Ph.D., Research Scientist, Angela L. Rollins, Ph.D., Research Scientist, Maria Monroe-DeVita, Ph.D., Assistant Professor, and Corey Pfahler, MSW, Doctoral Student ncbi.nlm.nih.gov/pmc/articles/PMC3156844/

And, lastly, some helpful continuing education:

Rapid Resolution Therapy rapidresolutiontherapy.com/

Courtney Armstrong, LPC courtneyarmstronglpc.com/courtney-armstrong-workshops/upcoming-workshops/